BLAMELESS MOUTH

JESSICA FOX-WILSON

Blameless Mouth

by Jessica Fox-Wilson

ISBN-13: 9780615417486
ISBN-10: 0615417485

Library of Congress Control Number: 2010940376

Published by Everything Feeds Process Press, Minneapolis, MN

About Blameless Mouth

Can we teeter together, on the knife's edge of having and wanting?
In *Blameless Mouth*, Jessica Fox-Wilson asks this question, by exploring the
cycle of hunger, consumption and satiety. The collection traces the poet's
relationship with hunger from childhood to womanhood, uncovering
what it means to feel forever wanting. Her work also considers the
cultural legacy of hunger, through stories of starving children and hungry
women, like Hansel and Gretel, Persephone, Eve, and others. *Blameless
Mouth* illuminates the struggle of living daily with the contradictory
pressures to want less but take more and searches for satiety in a culture
that encourages insatiability.

Acknowledgements

For the past five years, I have held on to this manuscript and reworked it, until it reached its current (almost finished) state. Throughout these years, many of my friends have provided excellent feedback throughout my revisions and support throughout my writing process.

I want to acknowledge the close reading of several of my past writing groups, who encouraged me to continue working on these poems.

I am also especially grateful for the generous support of my professors at Hamline University, most especially Deborah Keenan and Roseann Lloyd.

I would also like to thank my parents, for continuing to remind me to work on my writing in my free time.

Finally, I would not have had the guts to publish this book without the unwavering support of my husband, Aaron. I am lucky to have him on my side.

"Waiting for Snow White" was originally published by *qarrtsiluni*.

An early version of "Juvenile Delinquents" was published by *Poetry Motel*.

For Aaron, who has been a generous writing partner and tireless supporter, as well as a great husband.

Table of Contents

Eviction

Echolalia

The blank shapes blurred before the perfect man:
a photo out of focus, a world obscured

beneath blue waves. He began to babble words,
gold light became sun, brown lines became land,

gray fluttering hearts turned into birds, now
forever after. All his Father made,

he named, erased their easy edges, traced
straight lines. Then, something new, an undertow

of need devoured him, wants he couldn't name.
The perfect man moaned new words, words not based

in God's idyllic world. *I need this space
inside me filled. Lord, feed this empty pain.*

He curled, a tight knot, rocked himself to sleep.
He dreamt of falling down holes, black and deep.

He dreamt of falling as the Lord reached deep
inside him, finding me, submerged

below his skin, awake and purple faced from no
clean air. He ripped me out of Adam, feet,

then curled arms, flattened head. Now, it's been said
that I was made from his rib. This is wrong.

No, I was made from that initial song
of emptiness, the first words that he said

that were not names, were not repetitions
of His words. He spoke me into being,

with words of complete sorrow, freeing
his body from their weight. I was the one

made to free him, not made to be his mate.
Though, in my telling, I still came too late.

Orange Trees

In the perpetual summers of childhood,
I lived alone in the shade
of our backyard orange trees.
I sat in overgrown grass, among swollen
bodies of fallen oranges, flies
buzzing in heavy, fragrant air.
I gathered the excess in my hand,
shriveled rinds loose
against the sticky fruit.
I placed my favorites on the broken
air conditioner, wedged on the gray grate.
With my white knuckled fist,
I pounded the fruit to pulp.
Miniscule orange fragments sprayed
on my face, in my hair. Blood
rushed in my veins; power filled
my little, shaking hands. Orange
fragments dried on my skin in the sun,
evidence of so much life
thick in my hair, on my skin.
I no longer live like this. I subsist
on supermarket oranges, sour
yellow rocks, hard in my stomach.
I miss the taste of juicy oranges
on my tongue, the feeling
of bulging bodies
breaking beneath my fist.

Eviction

Despite our cheap excuses, we were through.
Our credit had run out. Adam began

to blame me right away. *How can you stand*
there, silent? This is all because of you,
your reckless, greedy ways. I packed for light,
quick travel, took necessities, at first,

then grabbed the last few fruits, fearing the worst
conditions. Even then, as Adam cried
about the loss of home and work and God,
as angels watched us pack, I calculated

our rations, how long we'd remain sated,
how long the fruit would last. I never thought

about the years that lie before us, years
of silence and work. All those hungry years.

Ten Miles West From Here, 4:42 AM

Look out the window, now. Swish of red and white tail. Slips
through the cracked fence hole the last guy left broken, unfilled.

Sleepless father flips channels. Seamless, glossy, empty
fantasies of pleasure pass him by. Clutching, unfilled

little fingers twitch open and closed, searching solace.
Mother won't wake until she cries. Young girl's unfilled

sleeping lips ask the questions they can only utter
in dreams. This morning, her mouth feels dry, scraped and unfilled.

Six blissful drunk teenage boys swerve past earnest joggers.
Their early mornings, late nights feel memorized, unfilled.

The same small red fox darts across lawns, scavenges for
food. Her starved stomach tightens. Can she survive, unfilled,

staring into dark windows? Can the fox see her full
reflection, mirrored on concave skies, gray and unfilled?

Live Nude Girl

Me in the back seat, secured
by the snug
blue strap of safety belt.
I am still learning
how to read.
As we speed by signs
for bicycle locks and home
security systems, I mouth
the words. Words like
lowest and best, first
only and free.
They all make sense to me.
On the other side of Century
Boulevard, the words change:
all-night, hot, strong,
secret and free.
Still free.
Then comes the flashing sign:
LIVE NUDE GIRLS
with a photo
of three women in red bikinis,
smiling in a steel cage. Alone
these words make sense:
live – what is not dead
nude – unclothed
girls – young females, like me.
We stop at a red light.
I lock my eyes on the sign.
I am a girl

but not a live nude girl.
I study my body, a mass
of white, unformed dough,
hiding my future shape.
I want so much
to be like them, laughing
despite the cold bars.
I whisper to them,
how do I start?
They giggle, *Girl,*
it's only a matter of time.
Their bodies writhe; the cage door
swings open wide.
The light turns green.
I press my fingers
against the window,
watch them wave to me,
Come on inside.

Inside My Glass Coffin

My Life in Fear

Dogs, Age 5

My body small enough to fit beneath
their dripping jowls, just in smelling
distance. Their humid breath on my bare neck,
canine eyes sizing me up for a snack.

Robbery, Age 10

The handle beaten, dangling from the door,
head in a noose. Door ajar just a crack.
Television missing, cats quivering
beneath the bed. His footprints everywhere.

Discovery, Age 14

I drop my cigarette behind my back,
stub out the red cherry with my black boot
toe. My mother always smelled smoke, always
blamed it on my best friend, that no-good kid.

Rape, Age 19

I am not afraid of the act, sealing
my eyes to his breath, his touch. I am scared
of my body after: a broken into
house, his fingerprints all over my skin.

Driving, Age 20

My first drive in rain: instructor urging
me towards the waving center line, cars
speeding past. *Don't be afraid of moving
cars,* he said, *but the ones who can't move away.*

Evolution, Age 23

Soon, my mouth will go, saying *Wait until
you have kids of your own.* Then my low back
will ache. My inherited Jewish knees,
myopic eyes already betray me.

Desertion, Age 26

My body has grown accustomed to him.
Can't sleep in an empty bed, can't open
sticky jelly jars. I cannot live in
a still house, only my body inside.

My Grandmother Always Used the Same Tea Bag Twice

Same porcelain tea cup, purple iris on the side
rinsed clean then filled
with boiling water, one bag of Earl Grey
at the bottom, kitchen quiet as the tea's color built

to black, like a patient, sleeping virus
or hidden inner eye of an iris,
the only moment in the morning she sat still.

She suspended the bag above her cup, set it to the side
of her saucer, a crumpled, forgotten bloom
until the next bath of boiling water, then compressed
against the curve of her spoon, the rest

of the color released, the second cup filled
with bitter, fragrant black. She willed
this simple sacrifice. On this loss, her day was built.

Waiting for Snow White

I waited in line for the ride when it happened,
swallowed in a thick red stream of sweating, sunburned
tourists. We stood in tight clumps, discussing the wait,

the heat wave, the first time we heard this fairy tale's
true ending. I peered past other bodies, straining
to see the bow in her hair, her permanently

smiling lips, the curves in her plasticine body,
modestly disguised in stiff folds of molded blue
fabric. A glimpse of red caught my eye, the apple

she balanced in her right hand. I wanted to pluck
the plaster, painted fruit out of her open palm,
cool my flushed cheek against its artificial skin.

Instead, we trickled slowly forward and a new,
sticky red trail ran down the inside of my leg.

Snapshot of Our Father: Swap Meet

His fingers
stroked the vinyl backpacks,
dented cans of generic

dog food. He studied
stitching on socks, pulled
peeling logos off purses.

We'd trail our father,
our small footsteps
fitting his own, in aisles

and aisles of hand-me-down
T-shirts and bulk detergent.
His eyes glowed, from want

of things. I'd find
the hollow Barbie dolls
sold without

clothes, you'd ride
the warped skateboards
with rusty wheels. We dared

not touch what we really
wanted. We always asked
for one treat: a sugar

coated churro, a pack
of yellow yo-yos. *Anything*
he'd say, *for you.*

Counterpart

He didn't want to dig

               this hole, alone

with only two

               cupped hands. The ground, bone-dry

and fine, slid through His fingers,

                    left behind

brown gritty dust.

              Of course, there was no one

around to dig for him, which only made

Him burrow faster, harder.

                Silence all

around Him, except His digging.

                  He crawled

along the ground, grabbed fistfuls

                 of earth, lay

inside. His great creation:

              hole the shape

and size of His despair,

               same shape and size

as His body.

          Outside, His hole, the piles

of earth now formed His shape.

                  Same lonely face,

same eyes –

          a mirror to reflect His own

blank shape: a perfect man to make, then own.

Model, Captured for Hours, Whispers

The photographer commands: *Curve*
your shoulders towards me. Scoop out
your chest. Silent, I comply. Push

my face closer to his lens. Arch
my delicate white neck. Contort
limbs into his positions. Hollow

that soft space between my hip bones,
until I am smooth and concave,
his clean vessel. I think of all

the hours I spend, scrubbing my skin,
skipping meals, sweating at the gym.
Making myself presentable.

I polish my body so thin
and mirror bright, I gleam and shine.
In the skin of shadows and light

stretched thin and tight across my face,
I feel what my pictures say: I reflect
everything you desire from me.

Inside My Glass Coffin

Shapes became distorted. Small watchful faces blurred
above me, transformed from solemn eyes, puckered mouths
into slender , dripping gashes, ravenous jaws.
I kept my eyes open. Watched my breath fog the glass,
then evaporate. At night, I pressed my fingers
to the cool lid, traced my name over and over,
just to watch it disappear. My arms and legs curled

inside my casket over time, confined to cramped
quarters. In my perpetual, clear reflection,
I watched my hair grow into black tangled vines while
my skin remained lustrous white, my lips stayed blood red.
Did she watch me then, through her own distorted glass,
as my limbs atrophied and my pure features froze
mid-bloom? I wonder what pleased her more, my dormant

beauty preserved inside her transparent tomb or
the day I was released, in showers of shattered
glass. After his kiss and my first few breaths of sharp
clean air, my life forever changed. I was no more
a beautiful girl, captured in her prime. I was
like her, a woman imprisoned against her will,
in her own fragile and perishable body.

Things My Mother Did Not Teach Me

Chopping apples on my cutting board, knife pressing
against the waxy red skin, I remember her

cutting apples for my lunch. Left hand gripping the
handle, right pushing the top of the blade. Our small house silent

those dark mornings, except for the sound of steel slicing
through soft, pliant fruit, knocking the board underneath.

She cuts halves, quarters, then eighths, dividing the core
in smooth, strong strokes. I loved the look of the pieces:

red outline of skin surrounding clean, white insides,
black seeds at the center. This is how I always

envision my heart, fragrant flesh protecting
six impenetrable seeds. Here lie my secrets,

my sleeping possibilities, my delicate
truths I never release, never allow to grow.

Next is the part I could never master. She grabs her silver
paring knife in one hand, a section in the other. She carves

out each minuscule seed in one quick stroke. Her deft
hands work fast, removing the heart. I know she's done

all this before. She wipes the remnants on the board.
Each sweet piece is perfect. Ready for me to eat.

Daughter to Mother

I never liked the flowers, translucent
pink petals, hollow
of the open blossom, slender
necks erupting into waiting,
hungry mouths, pistils
protruding patient tongues.

They all lay at my feed, asking
for sustenance
I could not give.

Then, the earth opened
into one churning angry mouth
swallowed me whole,
slid me down a
magma-slick esophagus,
held me
in its warm belly.

You would think it's cold
down here, icy as your rage. It's not:
we are full of bodies, compacted
against each other, warm
with vague memories of past lives.

They do not ask anything of me;
their mouths forever shut. I sit
on my black throne, gorge
on the sight of all

the heavy, full bodies. I absorb
every nutrient I need
from their forsaken lives.

Hunger

The mouth with thin dry lips, white slips
of skin peeling off.
The mouth with cracked corners.
The mouth that laughed too long, in that too
silent room.
The mouth that yawns wide,
a deep black hole.
The mouth that hates silence. Asks
too many simple questions.
The mouth that craves sweets at midnight, wakes
to raid the refrigerator.
Empty mouth.
The mouth that bites the tender pink inside
of her own left cheek. Sensuous mouth
that wears red lipstick, licks it off
before the night is done.
Mouth that begs
for dark chocolate, Merlot, and melted Brie.
Everything rich, warm, and completely forbidden.
The mouth I always feared
was too big.
The mouth I made too small.
The mouth I dreamed of rubbing off my face.
The stubborn mouth who never leaves.
That permanent, indelible pink stain.
Insatiable mouth that always asks for more.
The mouth that is hard
to keep open.
Mouth impossible to close.

The mouth that conspires, with me,
to keep us both alive.
Blameless mouth, who only lives
to chew, swallow, breathe.

Magazine Says: You've Worked Hard

I'm here to say you've got options. Let me show you
the brilliance of million dollar diamonds shining
on someone else's finger, the impossible

intricacy of hand-sewn lace grazing a girl's
naked calf, the smooth expanse of white skin after
hours of exfoliation. All this can be yours,

heft of clear precision cut jewels, whispery soft
femininity of youth, lustrous carapace
of perfect skin. But wait, there's more. I have dresses

for jobs you don't work, furniture for rooms you can't
afford, cars for streets you don't live on. Try this on
for size. Clothe yourself in the better things of life.

Wrap your body in thousand thread count cotton sheets
and you can be the woman, sleeping at home, wrapped
in thousand thread count cotton sheets. Not the woman

tangled in coarse sheets, at midnight, wondering who
she wants to be. I will do this for you, protect
you from the world, in our safe improbable dreams.

Juvenile Delinquents

Once we turn the corner, my brother and I
run ourselves dead, fleeing the scene,
though inside we were barely seen.
Our pockets are engorged
with Charleston Chews, Cinnamon Sin
lipsticks and Matchbox Maseratis.

The precious objects we seized
bump against our hips. We dream
of eating until our bellies bloat
and the chocolate leaves guilty rings
around our gluttonous mouths.

No one stops us when we careen
down the street. Our sneakers skate
unsteady on stray gravel and glass.

No one notices us bounce and bleed
our Hansel and Gretel trail of Skittles
the whole five blocks to our empty home.

Feeding Habits of Foxes

I show you scavenging
in decent people's garbage cans,
pacing behind a zookeeper's glass, loping
across lush green lawns. Hungry,
I never let you feed.

Why do I leave you
at the ends of lines, picking
at some family's thrown out food?

Another writer
allows you to ask
why you're not being fed.
Not me.

I know this isn't right, know
you hunt alone. You sink
into tangles of sun dried brush, disguised
in your matted red and white pelt,
invisible to your prey. Even now,

I can't bear to write
that you kill. In flashes of white
knife teeth, you kill to feed
your sleeping family,
to feed yourself.

I think I am afraid
of my own natural red hair,
point of my teeth, my silent
stalking ways. No matter

which cage I put you in,
I cannot escape
our common name.

What I Thought / Never Said

Right after we emerged from our cocoons,
dry husks as imperceptible as dreams,
I waited for Him.

Adam stroked the green
and supple leaves, protected his skin.

Soon,
I felt His cruel and heavy steps
crush thin new grass.
He saw us for the first time:

me
with pleased eyes,

Adam crouched
behind the trees.

The Lord could only sputter-spit,
You sinned
against my perfect world.

My brand new thoughts
burned inside.

This is where you've failed.
You built for us this perfect world,
then sailed away.
We were alone and hungry, not

from want of food. You made us,
just like You.
We're pure and perfect,
hollow through and through.

deep inside weighs

flailing

in frigid blue,

remnants of destruction

float past. she grabs what resembles

a broken piece of the ship. in the dark, everything

looks the same. instead, it's a safe, door swinging wide.

she crawls inside; she's just the right size. as she submerges,

deep inside weighs the notion that she pulled the first screw out

of the boards, just to see the ship crack open, the contents

spill out. sinking inside her black box, she finally

hits the bottom. her door opens. water

bombards her. at the bottom,

everything looks different,

blue shattered

glass.

Deep in the Forest

Zero

This one day (before there were days) there was
a darkness over waters, moist and warm
enveloping the world that was not formed,
sustaining nothing and everything as

a mother would, not knowing, cradling
her unborn in amniotic fluid.
At once a single sentence pierced through it,
an icy voice, precisely proclaiming,

Enough of this dim, placid, empty place.
I want to see. It was always about Him,
His flighty wants. A freezing bright light skimmed
the waters. Cold, brilliant, silver rays raced

across the surface, bouncing everywhere.
But in the beginning, I wasn't there.

Now, in this beginning, I wasn't. There
was only emptiness, then sound and light
invading space. I learned much later, night
was never like that first whole darkness. (There

are always His stars, spying, far away.)
After the light, He saw the world: a void,
an empty yearning to be filled. Annoyed,
He spoke, demanding life. With words, He made

the world. He shouted and white daisies, doves
erupted from his lips. He talked to hear
His voice, watch petals, feathers appear
at whim. He almost never stopped, in love

with novelty. But work had to be done.
He knew he could not do this all alone.

even if it existed, even if it enlightened

(going up)

i just want to be
closer to that gold
veneer that is my
sky, sparkling even
down here. every
day, i watch the light
filter through all those
miles of cold blue, warm-
ing bodies of fish,
castles of coral
and me. the sea is
so diverse, full of
spiny fish, sharp toothed
eels, waving green sea
weeds, oysters sealed shut.
right now, i must go
slow; careful not to
feel hundreds of pounds
of pressure pressing
my tiny frame. i
wonder what breathing
air again will feel
like, cold or burning?

(existed)   (enlightened)

i cannot recall   I would like to live
all the names of all   that moment again,

the people, men and   the moment i stopped
women, who told me   hearing my mother's

they would never leave.   tone in my voice. it
i cannot tell you   lasted only one

how many times i've   second. then, i start-
introduced myself,   ed wondering, fear-

how many times i've   fully: what if in-
seen my mother cry   stead of turning in

how many times i've   to her, i started
said, *never for me*.   turning into him?

Kitchen Door, Mid-Swing

Be-   tween
commercials   and programs,

he flies,   fetches
the apple,   the cola,

the bowl of popcorn.   25 paces
between den   and kitchen,

reclining   and walking.
He hurries   pushing with

his right hand   to enter,
his left,   to leave.

Twelve minutes later,   he remembers salt
for popcorn,   the coaster

for his soda.   Something's always
missing,   always

past his reach.   The door does
not stop,   swinging

open   and shut,
even as his pulse,   regular as breath.

One time,   when I
was a young girl,   watching the game

with him,
mid-

to catch the score.
swung back and forth,

of his ring
never saw him

swift sharp stroke,
he wants is now

there is the door,
hand. The TV

Led by momentum,
the empty,

he stopped
push

The swinging door
severed the tip

finger. I
cry before. One

everything
forgotten. Now

blood on his sliced
shifts to an ad.

he stumbles into
still kitchen.

Satiety

My mother at the time,
believed she was dying.
So, I served her
all the foods
she could not have:
pecans and cashews, Brie.
She consumed rich desserts,
Greek salads, mangos, green
stuffed olives. For days,
I chopped and rinsed, boiled
and baked. Bought
the things I could not make.
I watched her eat
across my own untouched plate.
I wanted to give her
so much more, everything
she asked for,
but I left it at this.
Right before her surgery,
she stopped, went days
without all food, drink,
until her lips turned white
and split. I think
her stomach finally felt full.
In times of terror,
I devour everything.
My body does not stop.
This time, her hungry, shriveled
body was my first repast.

I ate her pain, her cries
for blankets, ice, pillows.
I needed her needle
marks, her IVs, her glassy
eyes. I consumed her empty
black disease. I swallowed
more sustenance
than I could ever burn.

At the Heart of a Shipwreck

At the heart of a shipwreck
is a child

listening to the boards   listening to her parents

groan/scream
from so much
pressure.

At the heart of a shipwreck
is a child

feeling the ship   feeling her home

tremble/rumble
from some un-
seen catastrophe.

At the heart of a shipwreck
is a child

watching the boards   watching her parents

fissure/crack
from lightning bolt fractures,
finally break apart.

At the heart of a shipwreck

is a child

staring into a hungry mouth   broken boards/splintered teeth

shiver/sink

descend into black depths,

learn to breathe water.

Deep in the Forest

I.
Deep in the forest, you follow a well-kept path
swallowed by roots, mind its hidden turns.
You shiver at night, remember
the warm golden hearth. Think
of the last time you saw them, sealing
their front door shut.
You mark your journey

with your last precious possession. Your hands
smell like yeast and salt.
You whimper as greedy sparrows
gobble your only way home. Deep in the forest,

you hold each other at night.
You listen for wolves,
stiffen as the bushes tremble with predators.
Deep in the forest, you eventually stop talking
about Mother and Father.

II.
You spy a clearing, just beyond
the jagged tree line. You notice
orderly rows of cultivated plants.
You discover a home
built with you in mind. Windows are coated in syrup,
doors have chocolate handles. There are praline shingles,
peppermint bricks, lollipop garden stakes outside.

Deep in the forest, you cannot resist.
You nibble and gnaw, bite and suck, gorge yourselves
until your fingers swell, your stomach strains
and you cannot remember why you were crying at all.
I watch you devour and recognize the fury
of feeding appetites left long unfilled.
Deep in the forest, you sleep under the eaves
of an impossible house, dreaming of sweets your bellies

still desire. Deep in the forest, I wake you, gently.
Pinch your soft, succulent flesh. I offer you
nourishment you cannot deny and ask you
so little in exchange. Deep in
the forest, devouring dangers like me
wait for children like you.

Letter to Hunger

I close my mouth for you, hunger,
this one last time. Your bony fingers
clamp my mouth shut too long.
Nobody taught me to deny myself
better than you.

The local news showed me a mother
who left her baby daughter alone
for days, during a beer-drenched bender.
This was never me, but I see
the girl's tiny, urine-soaked body shivering
in her wooden crib, bars too narrow for escape.

This was never me,
hunger, but I've been thinking
about my childhood all day.
Full cupboards and empty houses.

Handwritten recipes for dinner left on the stove
ready for me to cook, before they drove home.
Brown bag lunches or crumbled lunch money, always
on the counter, every morning.

I know I never starved
for food, but for something else.
Something I refuse to name, refuse
to request.

I play this story
in my head. Pause
at places that seem both familiar and lurid. Cast
my family in these unforgiving roles. Her short life
was never my life. Her mother
never my mother. Her father, offstage,
nothing like mine.
I choose to play all these parts:
mother, daughter, father, crib.

Each day, despite my own packed cupboards
and my warm full home, I still choose
to deny myself sustenance
and something else too precious to name.

Red Lipstick

Each morning, I painted my lips dark red
with Wet N Wild, number 516.
I dreamed myself invincible,
as I blotted, pressed and powdered
until a brown-red stain

seeped into my skin. I turned
my music up loud, listened
to Rage Against the Machine,
and thought I could,
listened to The Cure
and waited for mine. In school,

I was mostly invisible, silent,
next to all the other girls with blue-red
war paint smeared across their lips.
I was just another one, cloaked
in black and skinny enough
to squeeze through the crack

in the high school fence. We broke
into our parents' houses, with keys
hidden in our Pic N Save purses,
punched in the alarm codes,
before sirens went off.

My house had Bud Light and nosy neighbors,
Elena's had a liquor cabinet
with Sharpie lines drawn on the bottle's sides.

We cracked open Cokes
and poured in whiskey and rum,
vodka and peach schnapps,
filled the bottles with water, right below
the line. We invited the boys
to watch them slam beers
and mosh to Metallica.

One guy said he went to juvie
for assault with a deadly weapon, pulled
back his bangs and bared his forehead,
where he bashed the guy's skull
open with his own. I laughed,
but left him alone.

One afternoon, Elena's dad came home,
found us curled on the couch,
drunk and watching MTV.
Her father screamed in Russian,
his face red and swollen. We snuck
out the back door.

The next morning, she answered the door,
slowly, wincing as she moved. Her nightgown
slipped to show her shoulder
covered in red welts. Her father
stood behind her, hand above her head,
pushing the door until it clicked shut
and I walked back to school, alone.

every detail tells this story

witness

                        just a girl
                        full of life and shimmer, just-
                        picked
                        juicy sweetness.

she knows
she

                        can be thinner and
                        more lightweight.

magazine says:
says:

                        allow us to clarify.
                        we have such control
                        of the product, here.

model,
whispers:

                        captured for hours,

                        she's born with it.

whispers:

                        it's complicated.

they both say, together:

                        don't
                        just fight, believe in beauty.
                        see pictures of her,
                        sexy but safe.

I can see we're both

                        surrounded, limited
                        by doses of the passionate
                        pursuit of perfection.

                              lines of demarcation form
                              down our middle.
                              it's not over yet.

I tell the girl: I want us to savor
                              nourish wild hearts
                              and our strong, silent,
                              subtle appeal.

magazine says: you've worked so hard.
                              you can easily manage,
                              however
                              and whenever you want to.

                              (you should forfeit.)

model smiles: I have to answer to no one
                              but men and my customers.

I say to the girl:
gifted daughter,

                              don't shed to be more
                              manageable. be brighter.
                              outlast.

she reads over my shoulder: how to steal this look.
reads: result: delicious.
reads:

                              we're only 99 cents each.

I turn the page,   like waving a white flag.

Learning to Love the Taste of Apples

That first, sweet, terrible bite tasted like
the sun's last light, setting on my green tongue,
like my first hearth fire, filling my small lungs,
like stars devouring blue fumes, burning bright,
like whispering words, wider than my mouth,
like thinking every thought at once.

                                        Back home,
my life was still the same. I was alone.
He brought home a butterfly, I longed to shout
its Latin name, its wingspan, its genus,
how long it slept in its cocoon, how long
until it died. Instead, I bit my tongue,

stayed inside. I longed to be like he was
that last night, as I watched him soundly sleep:
an animal with eyes closed, dreaming deep.

I let him dream that one last time. Outside,
I ran back to the tree, picked bushels, stole
His precious apples. My hands were so cold
and hungry, grabbing more than I could hide,

much more than I could eat. I thought
about the silence in our home, the words
that burned beneath my itchy skin. I heard
the serpent's voice in my head, hissing not
to worry.

Then, I made him breakfast, peeled
the red skin off the fruit, in spiral strips.
I waited for that taste to touch his lips.
And waiting for Adam to start his meal

was waiting for a butterfly to get
out of his cocoon, wings heavy and wet.

Womyn's Center Topless Spaghetti Dinner

Our preparations are intense. I spend hours peeling cloves of garlic. Not a natural, I pick pits in the cloves with my nails as I work to remove the stubborn, translucent white skins. My hands stink, sticky with an invisible film of garlic that won't wash off. The other girls stew skinned tomatoes, snap raw pasta in half to fit in the pots, slice loaves of French bread down the middle, drizzle melted butter and garlic. Half hour before, we undress. Some girls wear white bras or bikini tops. Others go nude from the waist up. Molly, Lori, and Donna flash gold glitter pasties they bought at Naughty but Nice, off campus. I cinch my mother's hand-me-down jeans below my waist, to embellish the curve and width of my hips. Molly paints a small, bright red heart over the center of my cleavage, as I cup my cold, bare breasts with my stinky, sticky hands.

During dinner, we never discuss our half-naked bodies. We serve each other streaming plates of spaghetti, garnished with fragrant whole basil leaves. We slurp spaghetti as tomato sauce freckles our chests, spills on our full bellies. We chew bread, sip glasses of red wine, and gossip. Some of us surreptitiously eye each other's bodies, in their natural and imperfect states. After dinner, Meredith and I nap on opposite sides of the living room couch, curled like kittens. As I fall asleep, I touch the dried, peeling heart Molly painted on me that night. It feels like an old layer of skin, lifting off my body.

Maenads

We were good daughters, once. Bent to the floor,
hand scrubbing your marble tiles,
hunched over the hearth fire, raking
extinguished gray coals.
Never breathing

a hint of complaint, never leaving
the confines of your homes. Laced inside
our coarse brown dresses
beat hearts of tangled roots, turning leaves
and creeping green vines.

All it took was one touch
from his pine cone tipped wand, one taste
of his bittersweet wine

and we were unleashed, running
through dense, drenched forests,
unraveling our tightly plaited hair.

We finally live without cares,
dancing beneath the wide, watchful moon
to the faint humming tune rushing
in our reedy veins. We circle
and twirl in one alive, laughing
mass, a tumble
of bare arms, half-drained wine skins
and soft, spotted panther hides.

Fathers, forget us.
We think of you, only in flashes,
after our long days of hunting

as we happen upon the one wandering man
waiting for us to pounce
in one sleek, hungry body,
tasting the honey sweet sorrow
steeped in his warm, vulnerable skin.

I Turn the Page, Like Waving a White Flag

I know you sold me, long ago. My purse
is crammed with receipts for all the products

you taught me to buy. The necessary
conditioners for my unruly hair,

concealers, minimizers, reducers,
all for my skin. Control top pantyhose

to squeeze my body into smaller and
smaller proportions. I spend my money

on miracle cures, potions, medicines
for a disease I barely remember

contracting. I wasn't always like this,
sucked so dry I need to buy slick lotions

to rub into my skin. I can barely
remember, years ago, my life before

all my purchases. I was once a girl
in summer, swinging on a wood swing set,

salting a slice of pink watermelon.
Juice dribbling down my arm even before

my first bite. I can remember how sweet
the fruit tasted, despite the edge of salt,

how it burst in my mouth, how I giggled
with my mouth still full. Where is my receipt

for that moment? I need to know. What was
the price for that young girl's joyful pink heart?

Living Next to an All-Night Grocery Store

I never know
what I really need.

I find myself, at 10:43 PM
craving mini-frozen pizzas, needing
three boxes of Band-Aid bandages.

I never wait
until morning.

I whisper excuses:
the cat needs more cat litter
my shampoo's practically two-thirds gone
just to haunt the wide, clean aisles, handle
fresh imported Chilean fruits, fill
my small orange handle basket
with chocolate soda, beef jerky,
and jars of marshmallow fluff.

I wasn't always like this.

I lived once
without my need for economy-sized
Suave shower gel and green Greek olives
waking me before dawn.

This happened, slowly.

One night, I realized, as I bundled up
at 3:22 AM to buy cherry flavored Chapstick
that living so close
to endless possibility consumed me.

                    I have memorized
                    the layout of the store.

I lie in bed at night,
grind my teeth, envision
the last lonely spaces
left in my cupboards. I feel them
open inside me and I wonder
how I'll ever fill them.

                    I hear the buzz
                    of flickering fluorescent lights

supply   supply   supply

                    Am I hypnotized?

I know nothing I can buy
will ever fill me.

                    I am satisfied

only with the possibility
of all the endless products
waiting
just beyond my reach.

Recurring Dream

I open my buried suitcase to find
my kittens, curled together
like question marks. Orange calico
head sleeping on a soft black belly.
Four pairs of paws flexed, baring
translucent claws. I place my palm
on their bodies to feel their fur, their warm
reverberations. Instead their fur pricks
my open hand. Their bodies feel empty
as eggshells or iridescent husks
of long dead insects. Then, I recognize
the signs of decay. Their pungent
death odor lingers in my nose,
my mouth. My mind winds back
to when I saw them last: the rainy day
we all played hide and seek. I zippered
up the suitcase that day, unknowingly
packed them away. How long ago?
Weeks, maybe months. How could I
forget to feed them, all this time? Each time
I open my buried suitcase,
I stroke their heads one last time, then hide
the evidence beneath my bed, or in the darkest
corners of my closet. I drift through my day
running errands, eating lunch with friends,
all the while holding a heavy, secret grief.
Oh, the wonders I once held
warm in my cupped hands, then forgot.

Betwixt

The Day I Learned the Definition of Lacuna

I fought with my mother about survival
of our species, long distance. As we argued,
I turned the pages of my American Heritage
Dictionary, scanned past labor
and labyrinth, laceration, lack,
laconic and lactate, to pin down
the elusive word that slipped past me
all week. She claimed

women starve themselves, instinctively,
to perpetuate the next generation's survival.
We can do without, she urged,
so that our children will grow strong
and live on.   I flipped my thumb
against the edge of the pages, fought

my instinct to scream. What about our survival?
Are we not half of the species?
She told me I'd understand once I have kids.
How easy it is to serve yourself less
so your child can eat more. She said,

I would do this for you, even today,
if it meant your life or mine.

I read the definition of lacuna
while we bickered back and forth.

An empty space,
a missing portion, in something
which is otherwise continuous.

I forgot what it felt like
to be the object of so much love
and pressure, to be the one who must
survive. I thought about my future life

as she described it, all the days
with missing portions. I saw
all the women in my family
who came before me, trimming the fat
off their own meat, slipping the best parts
onto a child's plate. All of them gone
and ending with me, a woman
who cannot imagine suffering
their loss. I saw all of this

so clearly right then,
generations of lacunal women
eradicating themselves, so I could survive.

Better to Eat Us With

I am the granddaughter who wears the red
wool cloak, braves the knotted heart
of the black forest to deliver you warm rye bread
and make certain you are still alive. I survived

the darkest places, where willows grow curled
and hollow as clutching hands and
hundreds of glowing yellow eyes blink back
at me, from inside prickly mulberry bushes,

only to arrive much too late. I can see this now
in the hungry yellow eyes and dripping jowls
in front of me. His hot panting breath curls
the loose tendrils on my bare neck and I know

I must make a new choice. Grandmother,
I spent my childhood in your kitchen, mixing
your recipes, kneading your dough. Your daughter,
my mother, has taught me well. Feed others

before feeding myself. Listen to your mother's voice,
not the voice whispering inside. Look at where
this has gotten us. You have been made
a more palatable meal and I am staring down

a starving animal dressed in your clothing,
plotting my escape. I can surrender
and become his second satisfying serving.
But, I cannot bear to live in his belly

with you, praying for some woodsman to deliver us,
whole, slick, and covered in blood, back into this world.
Instead I will swallow a hunk of our bread for strength,
shed my heavy red cloak, and run for our lives.

Betwixt

Two bodies sit, steeled
at the dinner table
on opposite sides, eyeing
one full plate. Both able
to stretch across, with plump
arm or thin, to dig in,
with their silver waiting forks.
This couple lives within
me, gaunt withered man and
his fleshy, greasy wife.
They take their turns, borrowing
my mouth, holding the knife.

Most days, I can tell who
I am, by the thick film
of bacon fat, lining
my front teeth, or the shrill
constant gnawing inside
my stomach. My face tells
the most, the gleaming trail
of drool waiting to fall
on my plate, or the dark
gray circles where brown eyes
once watched. I can hear changes
in my voice, the sigh

of rounded belly, whine
of sunken cheeks. This is
not my problem, careening
side to side, fat to thin.
I'm running out of room
here. I can feel each place
we touch. I grate against them,
knife scraped across a plate.
We have no middle ground,
no quiet place we meet.
They only leave me empty
plates, not enough to eat.

Legacy on His Disappearance

Without mother   without father   without fully

      stocked, equipped ship,   I am trying

to rebuild my   old home. In this   sunken, broken

      mouth of a boat,   with cracked plates, bent

silverware, all   this water rushing   in, uninvited.

      I have reset   the table, cleaned

water swollen   floors, removed all   hints of dirt. I

      have invited   guests: whole shining

schools of fish swarm   in and out of   my new home. One

      black octopus   has planted her

blooming body   at the table's   end. I am still

      waiting for my   reply, from the

sharp silver shark.   He swishes his   fins, swims sideways,

      watches me as   I sit to eat.

Lucky Explorer

I remember my heart
as a wild, beating thing
made of warm muscle
and motion. Memory
of pulse, lingering phantom
beating propelled me
a long distance.

Now, I've discovered
my heart, encased
in layers and layers
of accumulated water,
frozen, mid-beat. I am
the lucky explorer
who traveled all this way
to find such a perfect, preserved
specimen. In this cool, clear
sarcophagus, I see
all the evidence
of earlier times. With my sharp
tools, I shave
off each layer, each year.
My work is both
delicate and slow.

I rotate this fossil, carving
off the ice evenly.

I pause at each layer
in my carapace of my days,
cataloguing the traces
of what once tried
to touch my heart.
Stopped, mid-motion,
they all seem so small,
incapable of interrupting
my once-steady beat.

I examine each splinter
and speck, searching
for clues, the record
of what came before, what
comes next. One day soon,
when I finally
touch the center,
what will I find:

a wild warm muscle
recovering movement or
a cold red crystal,
clouded by intricate
icy designs?

6 Habits Filling My Days

Not Writing

If writing is like sharing a transatlantic
phone call with my muse, straining to hear her whispers
through crackling static, then, not writing is waiting
by my phone, praying *Any day now, it will ring.*

Other People's Accents

I steal other people's accents – friends and strangers.
Their lilts and rhythms roll and bump inside my mouth,
a dozen hard, mottled beige marbles. I have lost
the true taste of my voice, the texture of my words.

Wearing Black Eyeliner

I used to wear more. High school, 1992:
my eyes were two black holes obscured by my war paint.
Over time, this smudge diminished to a thin line.
Still protected. Just above my clear, open eye.

Crossing Streets

I walk against the stoplights. Pause, observe the flow
of cars and Mack trucks, buses and SUVs. There,
in the hole between the black Jetta and blue coupe,
there's my spot. Darting through the street, I claim my home.

Writing

When I was little, I saved change in apple juice
jugs. On blue, quiet mornings, while my parents slept,
I'd scatter sticky coins on my plaid quilt, count out
loud. Now I count syllables, mean as a miser.

Saying Good Night

After you switch off the light, turn on your left side,
I mold my warm body to yours. I say, softly,
I love you, baby. Good night. I feel our hearts beat.
This is not habit, but my last thought before sleep.

The Girl Reads Over My Shoulder

Everything in your magazine
has a price, whispered in small print,

hidden in the back. We can choose
which elements of the full page

fantasy we desire: blue shoes
with rhinestone clasps, five hundred bucks,

or the blue seaside she walks on,
wide and deep as open wallets.

You look at that picture and see
all the places you have lost, blue

oceans of your childhood, running
barefoot in hot sand. I see all

the places I have yet to find,
strolling on indigo shores

in elegant, high heeled shoes. Both
our impossible memories

are entwined with what we can buy.
They tell us, *Touch the leather and*

remember what you never had.
Ignore the insignificant

cost. We tell each other, *Cherish*
what you have right now, your priceless

beautiful life. We peel open
our wallets, offer all we've earned,

not seeing the vast reflective
sea, rising, right now, between us.

In Opposition to Heaven

Her First Taste

I came here, much too late. My perfect place:
a quiet clearing, cloaked in sun, a tree
with crooked branches, swollen fruit. I leaned
my back against the knotted trunk, tasted
the heady, listless breeze. Here, I forgot

my hungry nights. My nights with little sleep.
Nights restless fingers scratched my skin, from deep
inside my belly. Nights I awoke, hot
and twisted. Nights I prayed to anyone,
even Him. *Please let me help make this world.*

Here, I watched the sun, watched a snake unfurl
his form. He hissed, *You'll feel much less alone
with something sweet inside.* The fruit gleamed bright.

I'll always remember that first sweet bite.

related events

set one bowl, empty on a counter. count
each breath until you fill it.

sit down, alone in a room. count
each breath until you talk or move.

set two identical bowls, side by side on a counter. fill
one bowl with honey, one bowl with rocks. which
is heavier in your hands?

live your life in your body. on one good day,
how light do you feel? on one miserable day,
how heavy are you?

set three identical bowls, side by side. same
counter. fill the left bowl with marshmallows,
the right bowl with mud. leave the middle empty.
which do you hold?

after your good day, after your bad day, sit
alone in a room. count each breath, until
you cradle yourself in inadequate arms.

fill one bowl with water. find the perfect
place to see your reflection. count
each breath until you dip your fingers
in the water, blur your picture.

one morning, stand naked in front of a mirror.
count each breath until you walk away.

hurl your bowl against the wall. gather
its remains. count how many shards it made.

live through life long enough to be devastated. walk
through life, not feeling your fingers anymore.

glue together the shards of your bowl. re-
construct its original shape. fill your bowl
with water, watch the water trickle out the seams.

try to remember feeling whole.

In Opposition to Heaven

Coming to the top was not a straight bullet shot. It was tumbling
end over end, spinning like an atom. After awhile, I could not tell
which part of my body pointed towards the sun.

I did my best.

I eventually came to the top. It gleamed like liquid gold, even though
the sun was setting. As I somersaulted towards the surface, I marveled at
how impossibly thick it seemed.

I braced for impact.

I expected shards of water to cut through my skin. I expected cold air to
flood in my lungs, drowning me. I thought the sun, burning
in the distance, would scorch me alive.

None of this happened.

I floated on my back; caught my breath. Half of my body was still
submerged in water, trying to resist the undertow. I waited
for someone to recognize me, to take me home.

I waited a long time.

Finishing the Leftovers

Tonight, I will devour our leftovers
from last night's long, exhausting feast. Only
one spicy thigh remains, encrusted
with five hard, lonely kernels of dried white rice.
I cannot wait to pile a new plate high
with all our delicious indiscretions.
As my microwave hums, filling my room
with the warm aroma of allspice, clove
and garlic, I will remember sharing
our dish of blackened chicken, salty mounds
of rice and beans. I will feel the way you
looked at me, licked your fork. How my mouth burned
from all the spices. With the sizzle pop
sound of flesh warming, all over again,
I'll hunger for the heat that came before,
the fluid breathless moments that made us
so damn tired and hungry in the first place.

Hunger, Revised

Mouth, I now know you
are not to blame. All my life,
your sharp, insistent teeth
bite the tender pink insides
of my left cheek. Our cheek,
our restless, captive
teeth. Our life. I no longer ask
why we must break our perishable,
fleshy boundaries

but how we have survived
in this small space so long.
But then, I recall the tender taste
of first fruit in early summer,
the salt taste of skin,

and the delicious ache of wanting
all of these things. Sensuous mouth,
you have given me nights
of wearing red lipstick
and licking the stain off, before
the night is done

and I am through waking
with regret, the next
inevitable morning.

Can we teeter together
on this knife's edge
of having and wanting –

the blameless mouth and
the blameless woman

who wears you
like a crimson rose, opening
on her expansive, snow
silenced fields?

About the Cover Artist

Susan Sieber is a commercial illustrator and art instructor, working with both digital and traditional media. She grew up in California, has lived in Morocco and Japan, and received her B.A. in English from Beloit College, WI. Currently she lives in Illinois and is pursuing her MFA Illustration. In 2008, she was named an Illinois Artisan for her silk painting, and sells and exhibits her work at various Illinois locations. Her illustration gallery is located at: http://susans-art-portfolio.daportfolio.com/

About the Author

Jessica Fox-Wilson is a part-time poet and a full-time educator. She earned a Bachelor of Arts in Creative Writing and Middle-Secondary Education at Beloit College in Beloit, WI and a Master of Fine Arts in Writing at Hamline University, in St. Paul, MN. Throughout her career, she has pursued her twin vocations of unraveling poems and serving college students, with varying degrees of balance, luck and success. She writes about this balancing act at her blog, Everything Feeds Process (http://everythingfeedsprocess.com). Some of her poems have appeared in several journals, including Gin Bender, Blind Man's Rainbow and qarrtsiluni and her articles about poetry and literature have appeared in Read Write Poem and the Uptown Neighborhood News. She lives in Minneapolis with her husband.